His Grace Is Sufficient, His Mercy Everlasting:

Draw Near To God And He Will Draw Near To You

E. M. Thibou

TABLE OF CONTENTS

INTRODUCTION

There is nothing mystical or magical that you will learn here about what it takes to draw near to God. In fact you have probably heard it before.

If you have been newly converted to Christ you will find the information very useful if you apply it. Getting to know God for yourself is one of the most valuable things that you can do as a believer. It is in knowing Him that you will be able to build your trust in Him. As you get to know Him and you mature, you will continue to develop your faith in Him. The more you get to know Him the more you will grow.

Remember there is an infinite number of blessings that the Father wants to bestow on his children. Believers can miss out on them when they fail to draw near to God.

If you are one of those believers who has struggled in nurturing your relationship with God, and drawing near to Him, this is another opportunity to remind yourself of some things that you need to do to get things moving. Remember faith without works is dead, so take action.

The content here can also be helpful for believers who think that they are in good standing with God. Even for these believers, it is Important to stop for a moment from time to time, do some introspection, and execute a thorough examination of their lives, to see how they can strengthen themselves in the Lord.

Believers cannot ever be content with their current standing in God. They must always be on guard so they can continue to resist the attacks of the enemy of their souls.

We still operate in a fallen world and are all prone to sin. If we are up, we can fall. To avoid drawing away from Him, our eyes must remain fixed on Jesus, the founder and the perfecter of our faith.

A believer who consistently implements the points outlined here will be able to start, or build, a more meaningful relationship with God.

Draw near to God and He will draw near to you.

GOD'S FAVOR

Saved By Grace

A very crucial thing for any believer to remember in a person's walk with Christ is that salvation is free. It is free to him who believes, but it costs, and Christ paid the ultimate price for our sins. When this fact becomes real to us, it can be the most liberating experience that we have. When you come to the realization that you do not have to burden yourself trying to measure up to an impossible standard that will finally make you acceptable to God, it can be like lemonade to the soul.

The Bible says that it is by grace through faith that we are saved. Grace, being the unmerited favor of God means that we do not have to earn God's favor in order to be accepted by Him. We can never earn grace. That would be an oxymoron. God freely gives it to us! Working in concert with grace is the mercy of God. In the case of God's mercy, he freely lavishes it on us by withholding his wrath, which we do deserve.

How wonderful indeed is our God! His grace we do not deserve. His wrath we do deserve, but he does the exact opposite, and pours each out in abundance to all those who trust in Christ. Does this mean that because we are saved by grace we do not have to pay attention to our behavior? Of course not! We who are in Christ are dead to sin.

Paul addressed this issue when he wrote to the Roman Church. He asked this question of them: "What shall we say then? Are we to continue in sin that grace may abound? By no means! How can we who died to sin still live in it? Do you not know that all of us who have been baptized into Christ Jesus were baptized into his death? We were buried therefore with Him by baptism into death, in order that, just as Christ was raised from the dead by the glory of the Father, we too might walk in newness of life," Romans 6:1-4.

People who trust in God believe that Christ died for their sins to reconcile them to God. They trust in Him for eternal salvation and are now brand-new creatures in Christ. Christ imbues the believer with new life, and he changes the individual from the inside out. As God's children yield themselves to God, and because of the work that Christ does on the inside of His people, they find themselves wanting to please God.

Where Works Fit In

It is not that we come to God laying our works before Him saying Lord here are our works, hoping that we are good enough to gain His favor. Quite the opposite is true. We come to Him with all of our faults, all of the grime that is stuck on our souls, all of the muck on our hearts, and we say Lord take me as I am please, with all of the crud. Please make me into the person that you would have me to be. That is when God begins His work in us, and we in turn begin to display the change that has taken place on the inside.

Now, does this mean that we will never struggle again with sin? It does not! We must continue to walk in the spirit so that we will not fulfill the lusts of the flesh. Sometimes after coming to Christ, we get caught up in the daily affairs of life. We get sidetracked from our spiritual life. Occasionally, it is the pull of the culture that distracts us. Sometimes things are running so well that we forget from where our blessings come.

This is a dangerous place to be because when we view ourselves this way, we tend to take our eyes off Christ. Life is good. We have it all under control after all. If we are in a place where everything is going well, we must remember that we are there only because God has made it possible.

As a result of these factors, our relationship with God sometimes suffers, and we often find ourselves struggling to walk the way that we are called to walk. In some instances, believers in Christ even find themselves walking in their old ways after coming to Christ and experiencing newness of life.

Paul in one of his letters, addressed members of such a church, where believers were dealing with similar circumstances. The church at Corinth found themselves struggling with many issues that have no place being associated with the body of Christ. In one instance Paul even addressed a situation that he says they could not even find amongst the unbelievers. One brother was sleeping around with his father's wife.

So how do we reconcile all of this with the idea that it is not our works that make us righteous before God?

The Apostle John in one of his letters said that he wrote the things he did so that believers do not sin. Even though our works do not make us righteous before God, it is expected that we walk in Christ's righteousness. When we fail to do this we incur God's displeasure. We should feel dissatisfied, and ashamed in our spirits when we fail to live up to God's standards. It should tear at our hearts because as the scriptures say, anyone who walks in the flesh cannot please God. Now, displeasing our maker, the redeemer of our souls should cause us much discomfort.

Be Reconciled to God

So what do we need to do when we realize that our lives are not in synch with the expectations of our calling? In those moments we must recognize that merely trying to correct our behavior is not the way to go. Recognize that human effort to "do the right thing" is not sufficient. We must turn our eyes to the finished work of Jesus Christ, and realize that the righteousness of Christ is why we have been accepted by God in the first place. When our hearts convict us, that recognition should lead us to humble ourselves in a spirit of brokenness, and contrition before God. That should then lead us to reconciliation through Christ.

Do as the scripture says and draw near to God so that he will draw near to us.

We draw near to God when we engage with Him, and seek His guidance. Ask God for His direction. Desire and pursue fellowship with Him through prayer and the reading of His word. David said "Your word is a lamp for my feet and a light to my path," Psalm 119:105. In another scripture he said "Your word have I hid in my heart so I may not sin against you," Psalm 119:11.

The Apostle John reconfirmed the importance of God's word when he said he wrote the things he did so that we do not sin. He also said that if we do sin we must remember that Jesus stands as our advocate before God on our behalf.

Sometimes it is possible to get to a state where we have allowed earthly desires to take such a prominent space in our lives, that we find ourselves yielding more and more to the world. When John addressed the church in 1 John, he made it very clear that whosoever is a friend of the world is the enemy of God. We do not want to find ourselves being at enmity with God. When believers allow themselves to stray too far from God, they can find themselves in a place where yielding to temptation becomes more desirous. The Spirit and the word of God continues to appeal to them and remind them that those who walk in the flesh cannot please God.

Believers must never allow themselves to become so overwhelmed by guilt if they do find themselves in that position. When they slip, they should not let guilt keep them away from seeking reconciliation with God. When the Holy Spirit convicts us of sin that is a good thing. When He does, it is not to condemn us. We should not dwell on it by feeling sorry for ourselves and drowning in guilt. It should lead us to repentance.

Recognize sin, acknowledge it and run before our merciful father who stands ready to forgive us for Christ's sake. We have an advocate who stands before God on our behalf. Have faith in God and trust Him to make us into who He called us to be.

DRAWING NEAR TO GOD

Check Yourself

James the Apostle, in addressing some members of the church in exile said, "You ask and do not receive, because you ask wrongly, to spend it on your passions. You adulterous people! Do you not know that friendship with the world is enmity with God? Therefore whoever wishes to be a friend of the world makes Himself an enemy of God. Or do you suppose it is to no purpose that the Scripture says, 'He yearns jealously over the spirit that he has made to dwell in us'? But He gives more grace. Therefore it says, 'God opposes the proud, but gives grace to the humble.' Submit yourselves therefore to God. Resist the devil, and he will flee from you. Draw near to God, and He will draw near to you. Cleanse your hands, you sinners, and purify your hearts, you double-minded. Be wretched and mourn and weep. Let your laughter be turned to mourning and your joy to gloom. Humble yourselves before the Lord, and He will exalt you," James 4:3-11.

Faith and Works

The people of God to whom James was writing were infected by elements of the world's culture, and the lives they were living did not reflect the high calling of Jesus Christ. The letter of James addressed head on, many of the issues that the church was failing to live up to at the time. He did not sugar coat what he had to say and his rebuke was sharp. The book of James deals to a large extent with what some Bible teachers describe as practical Christianity.

James emphasizes that faith is not just something that exists in the mind, and demonstrated in an abstract manner by deep feelings within the individual believer. No, faith to the believer is more than just an intellectual acceptance of a system of belief. Faith is not just about feelings. More than that, but working hand in hand; faith in Christ is believing who Jesus said He is because He demonstrated it in the life He lived, His death, and His resurrection for the sins of the world. Faith is a commitment to live a life that is consistent with that belief.

The epistle from James deals largely with how the Christian demonstrates his faith, not in the things that individuals say, but in practical demonstrable ways. James emphasizes the all-encompassing reach of faith by showing how it affects our daily lives in every area. The letter covers a wide range of topics that have to do with practical Christian living.

James drives the point home that we have an obligation to live the way that Christ called us to live. He stresses that belief in Christ and His finished work for our sins is the only thing necessary for salvation. That belief will be reflected in the way that Christians live. James says demons also believe and they shudder. He then scolded the believers for their behavior because it did not reflect the life of the believer in Christ. He challenged them to draw near to God because being in close communion and relationship with God is how God will begin to work in their lives, enabling their works to match their faith in Christ.

The word (Watch Your Companions)

Drawing near to God involves getting into His word. King David said "Blessed is the man who walks not in the counsel of the wicked, nor stands in the way of sinners, nor sits in the seat of scoffers; but his delight is in the law of the LORD, and on His law he meditates day and night. He is like a tree planted by streams of water that yields its fruit in its season, and its leaf does not wither. In everything that he does, he prospers," Psalm 1:1-3. In these verses by the psalmist, he talks about the company that we keep as believers.

It is important for Christians to surround themselves with brothers and sisters in Christ who will help them to grow and develop into the people that God calls them to be in Christ. God's people are supposed to encourage and build up each other so that we can serve God with a clear conscience. Believers are to avoid the wisdom of the world, which is often contrary to the ways of Christ. Of course there are areas of expertise that at times followers of Christ may need to seek from non-believers. Overall though we have to be careful seeking the counsel of ungodly men, because the world consists of the lusts of the flesh, the lusts of the eyes and the pride of life. These are all hostile to Christ.

The Christian life is contrary to the culture, and disciples of Christ must look within their own assemblies to find good counsel about pursuing the pathway that God has laid out for

His people to follow. Not only must the Christian avoid the counsel of the ungodly, but he must not stand in the way of sinners, nor sit in the seat of the scornful. The Christian should not become too comfortable residing in their midst.

This does not mean that believers cannot associate with unbelievers. We know that Jesus did not come for the righteous, but to bring sinners to repentance, so it is not our place to treat the ungodly with contempt. We are not to shun them. What we cannot do is allow them and their way of life to be so influential, that we find ourselves drifting away from the truth of the gospel, or walking in a manner that does not illustrate our commitment to Christ.

Paul in his letter to the Corinthians puts it this way. He says "Do not be misled, bad company corrupts good character," 1 Corinthians 15:33. Another scripture says "Like a muddied spring or a polluted fountain, is a righteous man who gives way before the wicked," Proverbs 25:26. We are to be the light of the world and not the other way around. The darkness of the world is not supposed to overtake our lives. The book of proverbs is filled with lots of nuggets on how to avoid the negative influence of the world in our lives. Anyone who reads the book of proverbs will know without a doubt what it is to not walk in the counsel of the ungodly nor stand in the way of sinners just as the Psalm says.

Delight in the Word

Spending time in the word of God (meditating in His law day and night), like David says is a very important step in drawing near to God. When Paul wrote his first letter to Timothy he said all scripture is breathed out by God and is profitable for teaching, for reproof, for correction, and for training in righteousness, that the man of God may be competent, equipped for every good work, 2 Timothy 3:16-17.

The Christian who wants to draw near to God does not have a choice. He must delight in God's word. She must make it a point to meditate on the scriptures and let them take root in her heart. Getting to the place where this is the reality in a believer's life does not happen by chance. It takes discipline and a concerted effort to dig into God's word to glean from it the gems that God wants to reveal.

Coming to the place where one delights in the word of God is not accomplished by casually reading the scriptures, and not diving deeper than the surface. Paul also said to Timothy "do your best to present yourself to God as one approved, a worker who has no need to be ashamed, rightly handling the word of truth," 2 Timothy 2:15. In this scripture, Paul is saying that as people called by God, God's servants must strive to apply themselves whole heartedly to the things of God.

God has chosen believers for His kingdom and expects them all to live lives that are fully committed to Him, by obeying His word, and doing all that He asks them to do. As laborers with God, believers must ensure that they are not workmen who will be ashamed. The way that we ensure we are not ashamed is by rightly handling God's word as Paul said to Timothy. Believers must learn it, love it, and live it.

Learning to delight ourselves in God's word is not just an intellectual experience where we fill our heads with knowledge that makes us feel pleased with ourselves. By delighting ourselves in God's word, we learn to delight ourselves in God because His word points to Him. God's word highlights His mercy, His grace, His love, His justice and all of God's attributes.

When God reveals Himself to believers in that way, it tends to evoke a natural response of love, gratitude, and worship. When Christians delight themselves in God's word, they will be like trees planted by streams of water resulting in fruitful lives that please God. God's word is like a dependable source of water. A tree planted next to the river will never be in danger of drying up, or be unfruitful because of the readily available source of water that is always accessible to it. So too it is for the person who heeds the word of the Psalm.

The Importance of Prayer (the Lord's Prayer)

Prayer changes things. We have heard that statement many times before. Prayer is another important tool that helps us to draw closer to God. God's people communicate with God through prayer. In establishing that connection with him, there is the potential to affect our lives in ways that benefit us we probably never thought. Jesus said "If ye then, being evil, know how to give good gifts unto your children, how much more shall your Father which is in heaven give good things to them that ask him?" Matthew 7:11. From this scripture, some may view God as a sort of "cosmic vending machine" as one person so aptly described it.

We have to be careful. That is not the intent of Jesus' words to us. He is not saying that everytime we come to him in prayer for stuff that he will be dishing out goodies. God does want to bless us. He does want to take care of our needs, but very often we may have the wrong idea of what it means to be blessed by him, or even what we need. More than anything we need to prayer for God's will in our lives.

The main thing about prayer is not getting to ask God for things. That is important, and as noted before; God does want his children to talk to him about what they need. The main thing about prayer however is that prayer is one of the primary ways that believers get to build and establish our relationship with God. Getting to know him is whati it's all about.

Jesus taught believers how to pray in His model prayer. Learning from this prayer and implementing it in their own lives will help God's people to develop a closer relationship with God. Jesus said "Pray then like this: Our Father in heaven, hallowed be your name. Your kingdom come, your will be done, on earth as it is in heaven. Give us this day our daily bread, and forgive us our debts, as we also have forgiven our debtors. And lead us not into temptation, but deliver us from evil," Matthew 6:9-13. It is important to note that Jesus did not necessarily say to repeat this prayer. We can. It is not wrong or a bad thing to repeat the words of this prayer as a genuine reflection from our own hearts. But Jesus said pray like this. It is a model that we should pattern.

THE BREAKDOWN

Praise God/Thy Will Be Done

When we come to God we must acknowledge Him as our own father. Recognize His majesty, and that He is the master of the universe. Appreciate that He is God and that He is the source of our strength. Give praise to His name for his mighty acts. Worship Him for who He is. Bow before Him because the scriptures declare that He is a God of mercy, justice, goodness, love, and light. Praise him because He is deserving of all the accolades that humanity, and the angelic hostsbestow on Him.

Praise Him because he deserves it. It has been said that praise offered to God is like the lover bringing flowers for His beloved because he delights in pleasing her. Praising God is like cheering for the Olympic athlete who ran a 100 meter race in record time. When we jump to our feet and scream over the athletic prowess of a basketball player ferociously dunking a basketball, or skillfully making a three point shot all the way from half court; we are giving praise to men for things that cannot compare to what our God has done.

David in one of his Psalms expressed awe over the powerful greatness of Almighty God. He said "When I look at your heavens, the work of your fingers, the moon and the stars, which you have set in place, what is man that you are mindful of Him, and the son of man that you care for Him? Yet you have made Him a little lower than the heavenly beings and crowned Him with glory and honor. You have given Him dominion over the works of your hands; you have put all things under his feet," Psalms 8:3-7. Then he ends with the following "O LORD, our Lord, how majestic is your name in all the earth! Psalm 8:9.

David, despite all of his exploits as a great warrior, despite his majesty and place of honor, despite all of his accomplishments that were many; he could not help but to stand in amazement over the greatness of our God. Praise to God was David's response in acknowledgment of who God is. Throughout the scriptures are examples of God's people breaking out in praise to His name because they felt the need to express it to Him in response to how great He has shown Himself to be.

When God's people take the time to focus on God's attributes and who He is, it should give them a sense of wonder that causes them to give Him praise in return because He deserves it. This God is on the side of those who fear Him. Praise Him for His wonderful works. "Let everything that has breath praise the Lord," Psalms 150:6. Pray for God's will to take place in your life and ask Him to place it in your heart to accept whatever that divine will is, because he knows what is best for your life.

Our Daily Bread

It is God to whom we must look to be the supplier of all our needs. He is the one who blesses us, and there is nothing that we can do on our own. Without Him we can do nothing. All of our abilities, talents, and whatever we possess are gifts from God. It is easy to become so confident in our own abilities that we forget it is God who bestows his love, mercy and grace upon us to do the things that bring blessings in our daily lives. Some of us have been so blessed in our lives that we take for granted these blessings.

We get sidetracked by all the good things happening to us and forget to pray asking God to supply our needs. As noted previously, we have to be careful of this attitude because this can stir up an attitude of self-sufficiency in the believer. God wants us to acknowledge Him in all of our ways and for all of our needs even when we have plenty and feel that we have what we need to get by each day. In remembering to do this, the believer is reminded, and acknowledges that we have to depend on God for all of our needs. All that we are, all that we have is because of Him and the believer cannot ever forget this. When we have plenty and forget that it is God who supplies our needs, it can cause us to forget, and lose the sense of our need for God in our lives. We can neglect other areas of our lives when things are going really good for us in other areas. In following what Jesus says to "pray like this" we should remember that asking God to give us this day our daily bread is not just about food, drink, money, clothing , etc. Though these things represent our basic needs, we have other needs in our lives that we must look to God for Him to provide.

In praying that God gives us this day our daily bread, we are more or less asking God to supply our daily needs. When we do we must have faith that He will grant our requests. James says that "You ask and receive not because you ask wrongly, to spend it on your passions." Let us be careful to be not guilty of the charge that James makes against the believers to whom he was writing. Let us make sure that our hearts are in the right place, and not driven by selfish motives. Let us ask God to search our hearts and reveal anything improper that may be driving our requests.

Forgiving Others

Then there is the matter of forgiveness. We have all been hurt by others in our lives. The anger that comes from a false accusation, an attempt at character assassination, or someone trying to hurt us in some other way can leave us fuming angry, and wanting revenge. In those situations, we often feel justified in our desire to hit back and return the "favor" to those who try to hurt us.

Sometimes the pain comes from corners we never expected, or from people we never imagined would do us harm. An act of betrayal can cut to the soul, and cause us pain that we never dreamed possible. How do we deal with those who trespass against us? Well, we are called to forgive. It is not the easiest thing to do but it is what our Lord requires of us. How often are we expected to do it? As often as necessary.

Sometimes God does allow us to go through cerain trials with some specific individuals as part of our personal growth, but that does not mean however, that we do not have to be careful in our interactions with people. It does not mean that we have to keep putting ourselves in situations where others may cause us pain.

Forgiving is about letting go, and not allowing ill feelings to fester in our hearts toward those who hurt us. It is about saying no to resentment. God does not want His people holding grudges. Often it takes time and effort to navigate through the process of forgiveness, but we must never abandon the effort. God's people must learn to forgive.

Don't ever forget to include the whole issue of forgiveness in your prayers. Ask for God's forgiveness. Remember that He is the propitiation for our sins, and stands as our advocate before God to mediate on our behalf when we do need God's forgiveness. Forgive those who trespass against us. If as the prayer says, God's people fail to forgive, then God the father will not forgive them. As difficult as it may be, let us embark on the journey of forgiveness where it is necessary. We cannot do it in our own strength. God expects us to depend on Him, to seek Him, and pray for His strength that will enable us to make forgiveness a part of our walk with Him. May He guide us along this difficult path of our walk with Him.

Lead Us Not Into Temptation

Jesus said that as part of our prayers, we should ask God to lead us not into temptation. When we request of God that he lead us not into temptation, we are not implying that God ever does that.

This may be one of those verses where people camp out too much, and too long because of the way that it is phrased. A lot of believers ask, why would Jesus have us ask God to not lead us into temptation? Does God ever do that? Well, the scripture is very clear that God does not lead people into temptation to sin. Believers should not get caught up in the phrasing of this section of the prayer.

First of all let's look at what James had to say about temptation. He was very clear about God's role in temptation. James explicitly said "Let no one when he is tempted say, 'I am being tempted by God,' for God cannot be tempted with evil, and He Himself tempts no one. But each person is tempted when he is lured and enticed by his own desire. Then desire when it has conceived gives birth to sin, and sin when it is fully grown brings forth death. Do not be deceived, my beloved brothers. Every good gift and every perfect gift is from above, coming down from the Father of lights with whom there is no variation or shadow due to change, James 1:13-17.

This scripture verse should remind us of our own propensity to stray away from God, and the need to always keep our focus on Him. It should remind us that our propensity to sin leaves us prone to stray from God. Remaining conscious of this should cause us to plead that God keep us in the frame of mind that stops us from being lured and enticed by our sinful desires. Lead us not into temptation, but deliver us from evil.

Paul in his letter to the Roman church said "do not be conformed to this world, but be transformed by the renewal of your mind, that by testing you may discern what is the will of God, what is good and acceptable and perfect," Rom 12:2. We do not become renewed in our minds simply by sheer will and determination. It is God who works in us both to will and to do of his God pleasure, Philippians 2:13.

There is also another way to look at how the request for God to lead us not into temptation but deliver us from evil applies.

We do know that there are times when God allows us to go through temptation by the trying of our faith. For instance, God had a major role to play in the trying of Job's faith.

God had to approve and grant Satan the permission to go ahead and interfere in Job's life in a manner that would truly challenge Job's faith, like he had not experienced before. The Bible also says that "no temptation has overtaken you that is not common to man. God is faithful, and he will not let you be tempted beyond your ability, but with the temptation he will also provide the way of escape, that you may be able to endure it," 1 Corinthians 10:13. Satan was confident that Job would cave, but God knew different.

Every trial that God takes His people through does not end up in the same way that Job's temptation did. We may not end up with more than we had before. We may not be richer. We may not end up with more beautiful things, but God will ensure that we come out of the situation with our faith intact, and continue leading us on the path that he has for our lives.

Jesus' instruction that we pray God lead us not into temptation is not a theological statement that implies God leads us into the kind of temptation that James talked about when he addressed temptation. We are to simply ask God to keep us in the hour of trial, to be with us in those moments when we face those difficult situations, and their seems to be no one to help and no way out of the circumstance.

The petition that God lead us not into temptation is a request that aligns with the will of God that we not be given more than we can bear. It is a request for God to deliver us, and not let evil have any place in our lives as we go through whatever trials He allows us to go through.

God never tempts us with sin, but He does at times allow us to go through temptation in carrying out his will for our lives. Jesus said to Peter "Simon, Simon, behold, Satan demanded to have you that he might sift you like wheat, but I have prayed for you that your faith may not fail. And when you have turned again, strengthen your brothers."

In this scripture we see that Jesus prayed Peter's faith would not fail. In the same way we must pray that God would keep us when we are being tried, and the pressure to succumb to the wiles of the devil is great. There are times also when the pressure of a situation may be so great that we ask God to remove it completely, just like Jesus did when he prayed that God would remove the temptation he was about to face. He said "Father remove this cup from me, nevertheless not my will but thy will be done," Luke 22:42. In the case of Jesus, it was God's will for Him to go through the trial that was ahead. God may choose to remove one of yours.

In our case, when we pray that God lead us not into temptation, he may see it fit to remove it from us. Other times he may choose not to do it. In the end, it does not matter what the nature of the temptation may be. It may be the kind that we tend to bring on ourselves because of the pull of sin in our lives. On the other hand, it may be the trials that God sometimes allow us to go through for whatever reason He has in His mind. To be delivered from evil is what we ultimately seek. Let us not get caught up in the wording of the prayer, but instead let us place our emphasis on the substance of it, in the context of the bigger picture.

KEEP IT GOING

Continue in Prayer

As far as prayer is concerned there is even more to this important hallmark of our spiritual lives. At the heart of it all, remember that prayer is simply talking to God. All over the scriptures there are examples of people crying out to God at various times in their lives for many different reasons. We see people pouring out their hearts in times of distress, in times of uncertainty, in times of joy, in times of sadness, and on other occasion. Prayer is perhaps the most important way, right there, side by side with delving into God's word that the believer can use to draw near to God.

The believer should never, ever worry about "bothering" God. God invites us to come to Him. He delights in His people coming to Him with their requests, whatever they may be.

It is a good idea on a daily basis to set aside a time of prayer and digging into the scriptures. Doing this will give believers a sense of commitment, and will help them to exercise the discipline that is necessary to achieve the goal of spending more time with God.

It is common knowledge that dedicating a set time to a task instead of leaving an open ended timeline to accomplish it, makes people more inclined to complete the action that has a dedicated time set aside for it. It is useful to take the same approach to prayer.

Never get discouraged if you fail to adhere to the timeline that you set aside for prayer. Sometimes people get so frustrated with themselves when they fail to live up to their objectives that they figuratively throw their hands up in the air and ask what's the use. Do not ever get to that point if you fail to meet your prayer time.

You may need to revisit the hour that you did set aside for prayer. Is there perhaps a better time that you can set aside? Is it simply a matter of discipline that prevents you from meeting it? Whatever the reason, confront it honestly and continue working on setting aside your devotional time, then stick to it. Do not let the frustration of not following through on your prayer time on any given day(s) make you give up on your goal of establishing a more intimate relationship with God.

Let us always remember to "approach the throne of grace with confidence, so that we may receive mercy and find grace to help us in our time of need," Hebrews 4:16. By the same token do not get so caught up in the special time that you set aside for fellowship with God that you fail to communicate with Him at other times during the day.

Remember that our God is the omnipresent one. He is always with us everywhere we go. We can reach out to Him where ever we are, and whenever we can. It does not matter if we are on the way to work or if dropping the kids off to school. Prayer is not some kind of fanciful   activity that we have to prepare for in elaborate ways. It is simply an acknowledgement of God, and then reaching out to Him with the words of our heart spoken through our mouth.

Go ahead and call out to Him when you are stuck in traffic after a hard day's work. Voice your frustrations to Him. Ask for the patience that you need to deal with the kids when you get home. Talk to Him about that issue with your boss, a colleague, or your spouse. Have confidence that He is listening to you, and ask Him to bring the comfort to your soul, even in the moments when life seem the darkest.

Whatever you do, never lose faith in God. "Whoever comes to God must believe that He is, and that He is a rewarder of whoever diligently seeks Him," Hebrews 11:6. Keep in mind that Jesus continues to invite us to "Come unto me all you who are weary and burdened, and I will give you rest. Take my yoke upon you and learn from me, for I am gentle and humble in heart, and you will find rest for your souls. For my yoke is easy and my burden is light," Matthew 11:28-30.

In the book of Isaiah, God called on the people of Israel to reconcile themselves to him. They had strayed so far from him that God told them to stop bringing their sacrifices to him. He said that their sacrifices and all of the outward showings of devotion had become burdensome to him. God said "I am weary of bearing them, Isaiah 1:14. The people of Israel had strayed so far from God, he said that when they offered their prayers to him he would not listen to them. God had had enough of them. Sin had driven a wedge between

God and the people of Israel, and he was about to pronounce judgement on his people because of their sin.

Despite Israel's fallen state, and their continued rebellion against God, what is very evident when reading the first chapter of Isaiah, is that God still desired for his people to turn away from their sin and return to him. As you read that portion of scripture, the emotion in God's appeals to his people to turn from sin is palpable.

Despite how far they had strayed, we see God still making his appeal to them. He still called on them to wash themselves of sin. He nevertheless called on them to make themselves clean. He invited them to come to him. He said let us reason together all of you, and me. Then he promised to wash them and make them clean, if only they would respond to his call. They never did as a people, and God did go on to judge them harshly, but God made continued to be available to the remnant of them who did respond.

The point of highlighting the situation with Israel is not to draw any comparison between their fallen state and when we as believers in Christ fall short. The point is to highlight the mercy of God. He was willing to forgive the people of Israel who had sunken so far away from him. How much more does he call out to, and is willing to forgive those in Christ who sin?

Noted earlier, but as a reminder, don't forget that God wants us to come to Him even in those moments when we have failed to live up to the expectations that He has of us. Never let yourself be so overcome by guilt over sin that you remain in your fallen state, griping about what a failure you are. We have all been there.

In the moments when we do falter, remember that the love of Christ surpasses anything that we can ever imagine. He longs for fellowship with us and wants us to know that we do not have to be separated from Him because of sin. The love of God is boundless and everlasting. Let us never break our communion with God because we feel guilty, or think that we are unworthy to come before God because of something that we have done. Repent and keep on moving.

Continue to Be Thankful

As we continue in our quest to draw near to God, never forget to maintain a spirit of thankfulness. The Bible says in everything give thanks, for this is the will of God for you in Christ Jesus concerning you 1 Thessalonians 5:18. The Christian life was never meant to be a bed made of rose petals. In another scripture it says "Do not be anxious about anything, but in every situation, by prayer and petition, with thanksgiving, present your requests to God. And the peace of God, which transcends all understanding, will guard your hearts and your minds in Christ Jesus," Philippians 4:6-7.

Granted, God has allowed us in the Western World to experience an unparalleled period of peace and prosperity for a long time. The prosperity and fullness that we have come to enjoy can distort our thinking. We are not exempt us from the troubles that have plagued mankind since the beginning of time. Many believers have grown so accustomed to having plenty, or lives of success, affluence and other blessings that they think they are entitled to all of these things, and it will always be that way.

Many have fallen prey to the prosperity gospel. They believe that their lives should only be filled with the things that many falsely believe are the only evidences of God's blessings in their lives. They subscribe to the belief that a Christian should always be in good health. They think that they are exempt from family troubles. They believe they will never have problems on the job. They believe that material riches are how God shows His goodness to believers. If they go through tough times they think that something is wrong with them. Difficult times make them believe that they have lost favor with God.

Sometimes hard times make believers think that they have no reason to be thankful, but this is contrary to what the word of God says. Jesus said "I have said these things to you, that in me you may have peace. In the world you will have tribulation. But take heart; I have overcome the world," John 16:33.

This scripture should make believers rethink their ideas of what constitute blessings, and the reasons for which they think they can be thankful. This world is not our home. It is broken. Sin has defiled it. There is dysfunction all around and it often touches the lives of believers. Because Christ has overcome the world, we will overcome the world. This should lift our spirits and help us to remember that no matter what our circumstances may be, we always have reason to express gratitude to God. We must maintain a spirit of thankfulness to help us appreciate all that God is working in our lives.

When we understand that God is in control of our lives, we will learn like the Apostle Paul to be thankful in whatever situation, or condition we find ourselves.

When God calls on believers to be thankful in the midst of difficulty, it does not mean that we are to live in denial of the difficulties we face in our lives at any given moment. It simply means that we understand who God is. He channels the course of our lives, and when we depend on Him in all situations, thankfulness should be a natural response.

Paul raised some very salient points in the following scriptures. "Who shall separate us from the love of Christ? Shall tribulation, or distress, or persecution, or famine, or nakedness, or danger, or sword? As it is written, 'For your sake we are being killed all the day long; we are regarded as sheep to be slaughtered.' No, in all these things we are more than conquerors through Him who loved us. For I am sure that neither death nor life, nor angels nor rulers, nor things present nor things to come, nor powers, nor height nor depth, nor anything else in all creation, will be able to separate us from the love of God in Christ Jesus our Lord," Romans 8:35-39.

When we keep these things in mind, we will understand the Apostle's exhortation to give thanks in all things. Be thankful when the blessings are flowing and manifested in ways that make us smile and jump for joy. That goes without saying. We do that spontaneously without anyone prompting us to do it, but don't forget to be thankful when it seems like all is lost.

Trust that God has everything under control, that he knows what he is doing in our lives, "And whatever you do, whether in word or deed, do it all in the name of the Lord Jesus, giving thanks to God the Father through Him," Colossians 3:17.

In reading the letters that Paul wrote to the churches, it is evident that Paul placed a premium on being thankful. We should keep this in mind as we go about our daily lives. Maintaining this attitude requires effort, but remember that "We can do all things through Him who is our strength," Philippians 4:13. When Paul said those famous words in Philippians, he was not talking about doing the things that people usually associate with that scripture. He was not indicating that everything the saints of God put their hands to will to turn to gold.

Those words came after he spoke of knowing what it is to experience good times and hard times. He was alluding to the fact that no matter what the situation he found Himself in (often really difficult situations), he knew that God would give Him the strength to endure. He could boldly speak those words as a result. "I can do all things through Christ who strengthens me," Philippians 4:13.

It is no wonder that Paul could maintain a spirit of thankfulness the way that he did, and always made a point of emphasizing the same in his letters to believers. In another exhortation he said "Let the message of Christ dwell among you richly as you teach and admonish one another with all wisdom through psalms, hymns, and songs from the Spirit, singing to God with gratitude in your hearts," Colossians 3:16.

As we seek to draw closer to God, the spirit of thankfulness must be an integral part of this effort to know Him. If we keep this in mind it will help us get to know Him better. "Oh give thanks to the LORD, for He is good; for His steadfast love endures forever!" Psalm 118:29.

Fellowship

Salvation is a personal thing. Everyone must know God for themselves.

When the chips are down and everything around seems to be caving in, believers must look to God individually and trust that God will bring them through their difficult moments.

Each person must develop an individual relationship with God, however; God does not intend for Christians to walk alone. We need each other to help grow, and build each other up in the faith.

To help us grow in Christ and draw close to God, it is important in the life of a believer to have a place of fellowship where one meets with other believers, "Not neglecting to meet together, as is the habit of some, but encouraging one another, and all the more as you see the day drawing near," Hebrews 10:25.

Attending church provides a great way for believers to meet with people of like mind. As human beings, we need the fellowship of others with whom we have things in common. We are social creatures after all. We need each other. Let's use this need to support one another as we all seek to grow in Christ.

David declared "how good and pleasant it is when brothers dwell in unity," Psalm 133:1. David likened the beauty of brethren having fellowship to the anointing oil that gets poured on Aaron's head. David says "It is like the precious oil on the head running down on the beard, on the beard of Aaron, running down on the collar of his robes! It is like the dew of Hermon, which falls on the mountains of Zion! For there the Lord has commanded the blessing, life forevermore," Psalm 133:2-3.

This image may not necessarily evoke the kind of feelings that we get when we think of something beautiful, but there was a lot of significance in this image for David and the people of the time who would have read it. In the end, all that matters is that the image was a thing of beauty to David, so much so that he wrote it down for our benefit.

We should cherish the beauty of fellowship in Christ. The relationships that people build in the body of Christ can help to strengthen each other in the faith. Together we all make up the body of Christ. We need everyone functioning in their individual capacity to function at the body's maximum effectiveness. A good Bible believing church where the people love God, and are motivated to serve Him is a solid place to help believers grow in their faith and develop their relationship with God.

The bonds that believers develop with the community of saints at a church with common values, and shared beliefs help give a sense of belonging, build confidence, develop strong friendships, and can help strengthen a person's relationship with God. There is strength in believers coming together to fellowship, to pray, to praise God, and to worship.

In addition, God provides leaders to help the people they lead walk with God, and develop their relationships with Him. These leaders do this by the example of their lives, and when they dispense the wisdom of God's word to those they lead. Finding a good church could be pivotal to a person building a relationship with God and drawing near to Him.

In Conclusion

It is a wonderful thing to say it is well with my soul. Jesus says "No one can come to God except the Father who sent me draws Him" John 6:44. When God is so gracious to us and pours out His love, it should make us want to know Him more and more. Getting to know Him does not just happen on its own. It requires continued dependence on the grace of God, and taking the actual steps to build a relationship with Him. It is not automatic. It is important for believers to examine themselves regularly to make sure that they are walking in the faith. It does not matter where a person thinks he is in his walk with God.

Even if it seems that your walk with Christ is on track, do not ever get to the point where you are too comfortable because you think you have it all figured out. The Bible says that we must "Be sober-minded; be watchful. Your adversary the devil prowls around like a roaring lion, seeking someone to devour," 1 Peter 5:8. We must always be on the look out to ensure that we do not get caught with our guards down even when we think that our relationship with God is on a good platform.

Those who find themselves struggling, do not lose heart. God continues to extend His open arms to you. Put your trust in him and do the things that are necessary to draw near to him. If you are struggling, get right and reconcile with Him. Jesus is our advocate.

It is God's will that His children walk in victory, not defeat. Remember that Jesus has overcome the world and continues to make it possible for us to walk in victory and relationship with God. God has provided all of the tools that we need to build our relationship with Him, and draw close to Him. Make use of these tools and let the process begin.

THE AUTHOR

The Author is a believer in Christ who knows what it is to struggle drawing near to God. He says he is as flawed as they come. He identifies with the words of the Apostle Paul who said that the things he wants to do, are the things he often finds that he is not doing, and the things that he does not want to do are the things that he finds himself doing.

Despite God's word providing all of the information that is necessary to live a successful Christian life, and the Holy Spirit's provision, he knows through this own experience that applying the information to his own life can be quite challenging.

Notwithstanding these struggles, the work that Christ did on Calvary and his spectacular defeat of death, demonstrated in his resurrection to life again, makes victory possible.

It is in placing trust in Christ, believing that God will do what he says he will do, depending on the Holy Spirit to lead, and diligently working to be transformed by the renewing of the mind, that drawing near to God has become possible.

The few pages of this book are not meant to convey the idea that the author has mastered "the art" of drawing close to God. He does not have any special insight to special insider secrets that will make drawing close to God a cake walk endeavor.

He knows firsthand that just like the Bible says, our enemy walks around like a roaring lion seeking whom he may devour. To not be devoured requires being sober and vigilant. The war for our souls is constant, waged in many battles meant to distract, discourage, and destroy.

It is in Christ alone, clothed in the whole armor of God, and depending on Him to walk in accordance with his will, can he draw near to God where there is fullness of joy, and at his right hand pleasures forever more, Psalm 16:11.

His Grace Is Sufficient, His Mercy Everlasting: